Curious Questions & Answers about... My Body

"You're curious too, so we want to find out about YOU!"

"What's your NAME?"

"How OLD are you?"

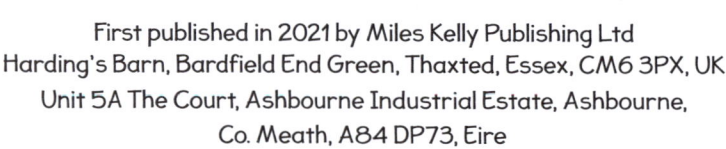

First published in 2021 by Miles Kelly Publishing Ltd
Harding's Barn, Bardfield End Green, Thaxted, Essex, CM6 3PX, UK
Unit 5A The Court, Ashbourne Industrial Estate, Ashbourne,
Co. Meath, A84 DP73, Eire

Copyright © Miles Kelly Publishing Ltd 2021

2 4 6 8 10 9 7 5 3 1

Publishing Director   Belinda Gallagher
Creative Director   Jo Cowan
Editorial Director   Rosie Neave
Design Manager   Joe Jones
Cover Designers   Andrea Slane, Mark Penfound
Image Manager   Liberty Newton
Production   Elizabeth Collins
Reprographics   Stephan Davis
Assets   Venita Kidwai
Consultant   Dr Kristina Routh

All rights reserved. No part of this publication may be reproduced, stored in a retrieval system, or transmitted by any means, electronic, mechanical, photocopying, recording or otherwise, without the prior permission of the copyright holder.

ISBN 978-1-83515-094-8

Printed in China

British Library Cataloguing-in-Publication Data
A catalogue record for this book is available from the British Library

Made with paper from a sustainable forest

www.mileskelly.net

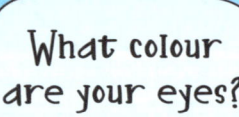

"What colour are your eyes?"

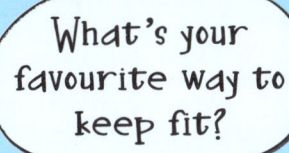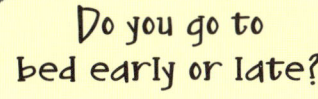

Curious Questions & Answers about... My Body

Words by Anne Rooney

Illustrations by Ana Gomez

Miles Kelly

What is my body for?

Your body lets you see, hear, smell, taste and touch the world around you. You can use it to run, jump, think, talk, and have all kinds of fun. Without it, you couldn't do anything.

Our bodies look different on the outside, but inside we all have bones, muscles and blood.

Cells make up tissue such as bone, muscle and blood.

Why are cells so special?

Because they are the tiny building blocks that together make up your body. Different cells do different jobs. You have blood cells, bone cells, skin cells and lots more.

Bone cells make up your skeleton

"X-rays can check for broken bones."

How can doctors see inside our bodies?

Doctors can look inside the body with scans and X-rays to see where all the parts are and how they fit together. They can even look at single cells with microscopes that magnify them.

Muscle cells help to form every muscle in your body

Your blood contains trillions of red blood cells

Why do I need to eat?

Food provides the energy your body needs to keep working. Chemicals from food repair your body and help it grow. Your body breaks down food and rearranges the chemicals to make skin, hair, bones and all the other parts.

Can I balance my food?

Yes you can, but not on your head! It's important to eat a wide range of foods from different food groups to make sure you stay fit and healthy.

Fruit and vegetables
Eat lots of these for fibre and goodness

Protein
Meat, fish and beans help your body grow and repair itself

What happens when I eat?

The food you eat takes a long and twisty route through your digestive system. At each stage, your body pulls out the good things it needs.

Always wash your hands before eating.

① **How do teeth help?**
Your teeth break up food as you chew. They chew it into smaller pieces and mash it around. Food mixes with saliva in your mouth, making it easier to swallow.

② **Where does food go first?**
When you swallow, food goes into a tube in your throat called your oesophagus (say 'ee-sof-a-guss'). Muscles push the food down to your stomach, squeezing behind the lump of food so that it moves along.

Oesophagus

From mouth to stomach takes 5–8 seconds

5) Why do I need to poo?

To get rid of the bits that your body doesn't need. These parts are squashed together and mixed with dead cells and water from your gut. They leave your body when you go to the toilet.

Always wash your hands after going to the toilet.

3) Why is there acid in my stomach?

Acid dissolves food into a gloopy liquid. Muscles in your stomach also churn the mixture around to break it up.

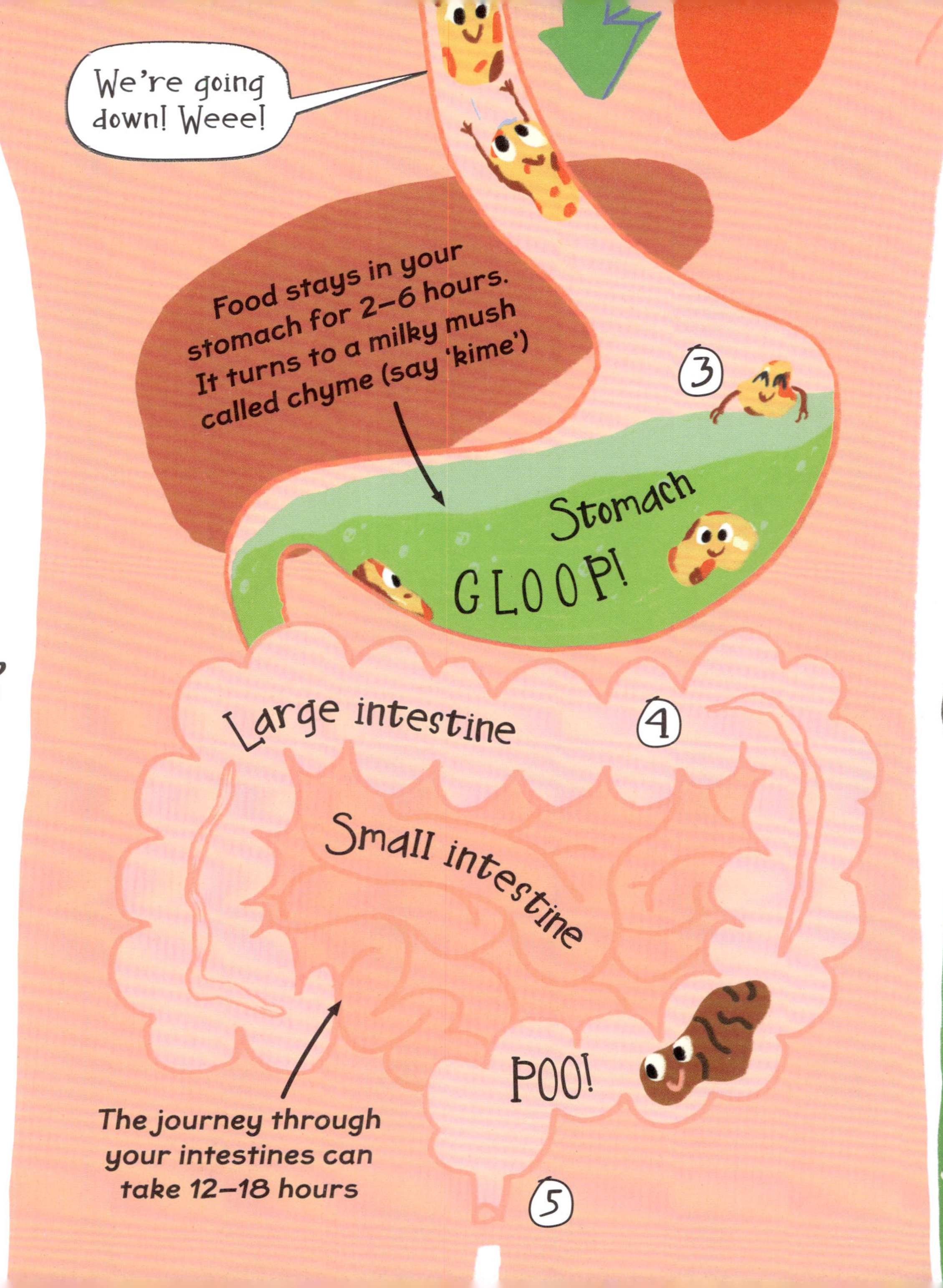

4) What goes on in my intestines?

A milky mushy liquid moves into and through your intestines where nutrients (useful chemicals) and water are absorbed. The leftover parts are turned into... poo!

We're going down! Weee!

Food stays in your stomach for 2–6 hours. It turns to a milky mush called chyme (say 'kime')

Stomach GLOOP!

Large intestine

Small intestine

POO!

The journey through your intestines can take 12–18 hours

What is my skeleton made of?

Bones form the rigid framework for your body — your skeleton. They support your body and provide somewhere for your muscles to fix to.

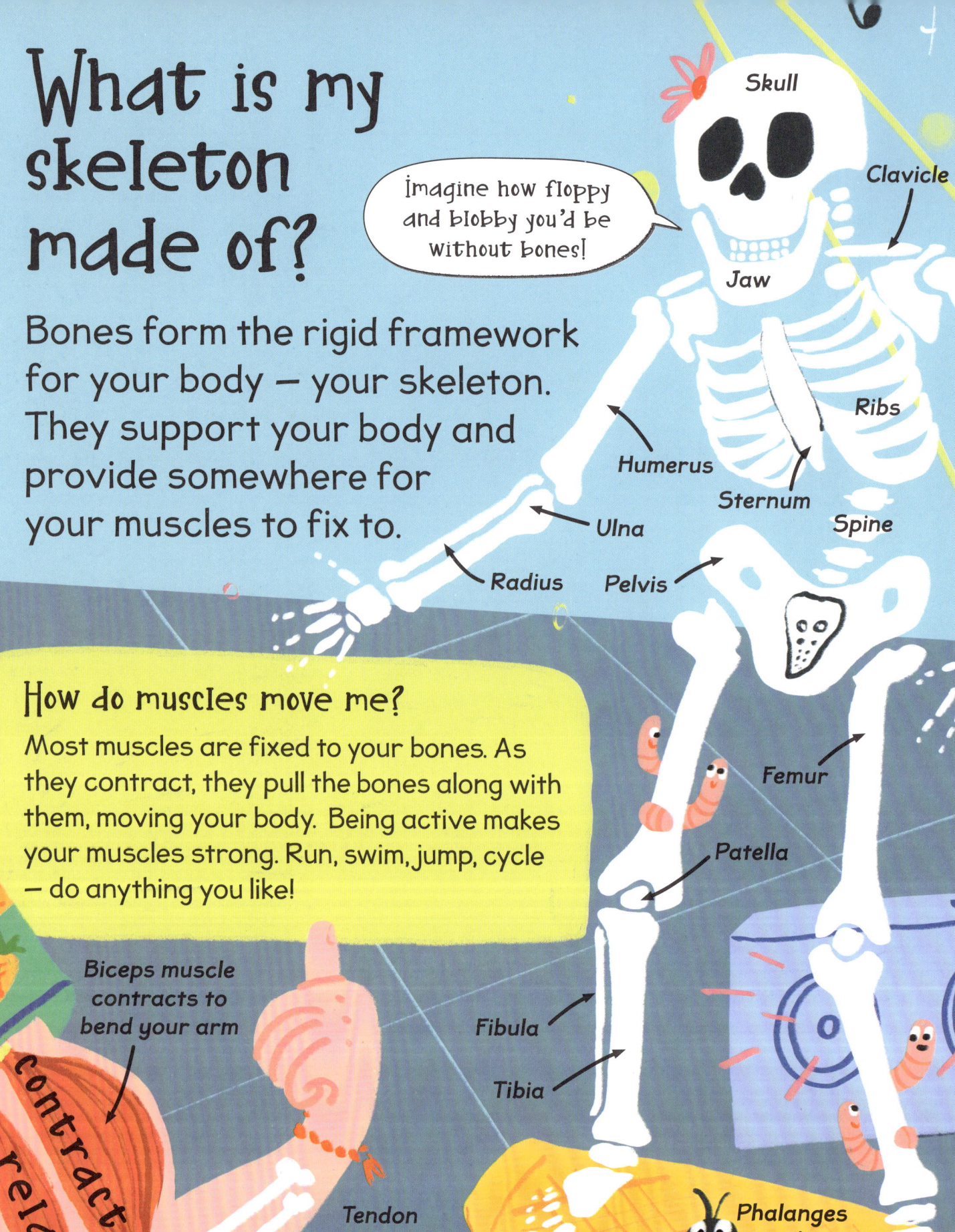

Imagine how floppy and blobby you'd be without bones!

Skull
Clavicle
Jaw
Ribs
Humerus
Sternum
Spine
Ulna
Radius
Pelvis
Femur
Patella
Fibula
Tibia
Phalanges

How do muscles move me?

Most muscles are fixed to your bones. As they contract, they pull the bones along with them, moving your body. Being active makes your muscles strong. Run, swim, jump, cycle — do anything you like!

Biceps muscle contracts to bend your arm

contract
relax

Tendon attaches muscle to bone

Triceps muscle relaxes

Activities like swimming make you breathe fast

Lung

Heart

Lung

What happens when I breathe?

When you breathe in, your lungs fill with air. Oxygen from the air goes into your blood and is delivered to your whole body. Old air is pushed out when you breathe out.

How does my blood deliver oxygen?

Your blood flows through tubes called blood vessels. These reach every single part of your body to make sure you have all the oxygen you need. Your heart and blood together are called the circulatory system.

Blood vessels

Why does my heart thump?

When you exercise, your heart beats faster to pump blood around your body quickly, to deliver the oxygen your muscles need. You also breathe faster to get more oxygen, and you feel out of breath.

Why can't I breathe underwater?

Because you don't have gills like a fish! Your lungs can only take oxygen from the air. A fish's gills can take dissolved oxygen from water. When you swim underwater, you need to come to the surface for air.

Why am I ticklish?

Because you have a sense of touch! Your body uses five senses to find out about the world around you. Your senses pick up information and send it to your brain.

Cells in your nose help you recognize smells — **Smell**

Eyes let in light to help you see all around you — **See**

Ears pick up sound vibrations to help you hear — **Hear**

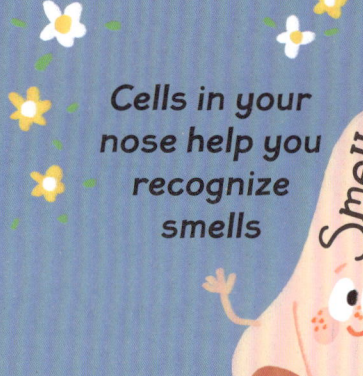

Special areas on your tongue tell you what something tastes like — **Taste**

Touch — Skin is packed with touch sensors to help you feel

Why can't I see in the dark?

Because you need light to bounce off objects and into your eyes. A lens in your eye helps focus the light, and a nerve carries information to your brain to make an image — and that is what you see.

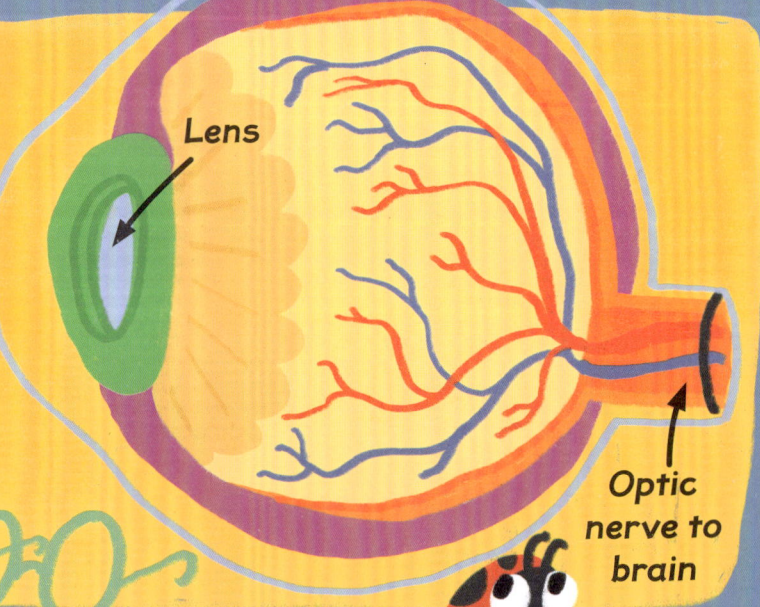

Lens

Optic nerve to brain

16

Why are ears a funny shape?

The shape of your ears helps to funnel sound into them. Sound is then carried inside your ear, where signals are sent along a nerve to your brain, so it can make sense of what you hear.

The outer ear is called the pinna

Soundwaves in

Tiny ear bones

Auditory nerve to brain

How do I smell?

Your sense of smell is produced by cells high above and behind your nose. Tiny particles of the thing you are smelling reach those cells.

Tiny cells detect smell particles and send signals to your brain

Smell particles go up your nose

What helps me taste food?

Your tongue is covered with blobs surrounded by tiny taste buds. The taste buds send messages to your brain about the chemicals dissolved in food, and your brain turns the information into tastes.

In **complete darkness,** your eyes could spot the light from a candle 48 kilometres away.

Some parts of your body are never replaced. The **enamel** on your teeth and the **goo** inside your **eyes** have to last a lifetime.

By the time you were six months old, your **eyes** were already **two thirds** their adult size.

Children can hear higher sounds than adults, including **bats** squeaking and **ultrasonic** dog whistles.

Fingerprints are not the body's only unique pattern. You can also be identified by your **tongue print**, your personal **smell** and the pattern in your **iris** (the coloured part of your eye).

Your **blood** is made inside your **bones**.

Is my brain in charge?

What you say, think and how you move, and everything else you do, is controlled by your brain.

It receives information
A network of nerves tells your brain what is happening to your body. Your brain is linked to your body by your spinal cord

Stand on one foot and spin the ball.

Brain

Spinal cord

It sends messages
Your brain sends messages to your body, telling it how to react or move

Nerve network

What do my nerves do?
Nerves are collections of nerve cells (neurons). They carry information between all parts of your body and brain. When you see, smell, taste or hear anything, information is carried by nerves to your brain super-quickly.

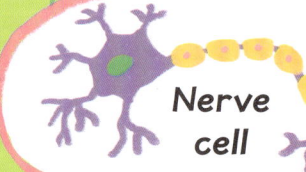
Nerve cell

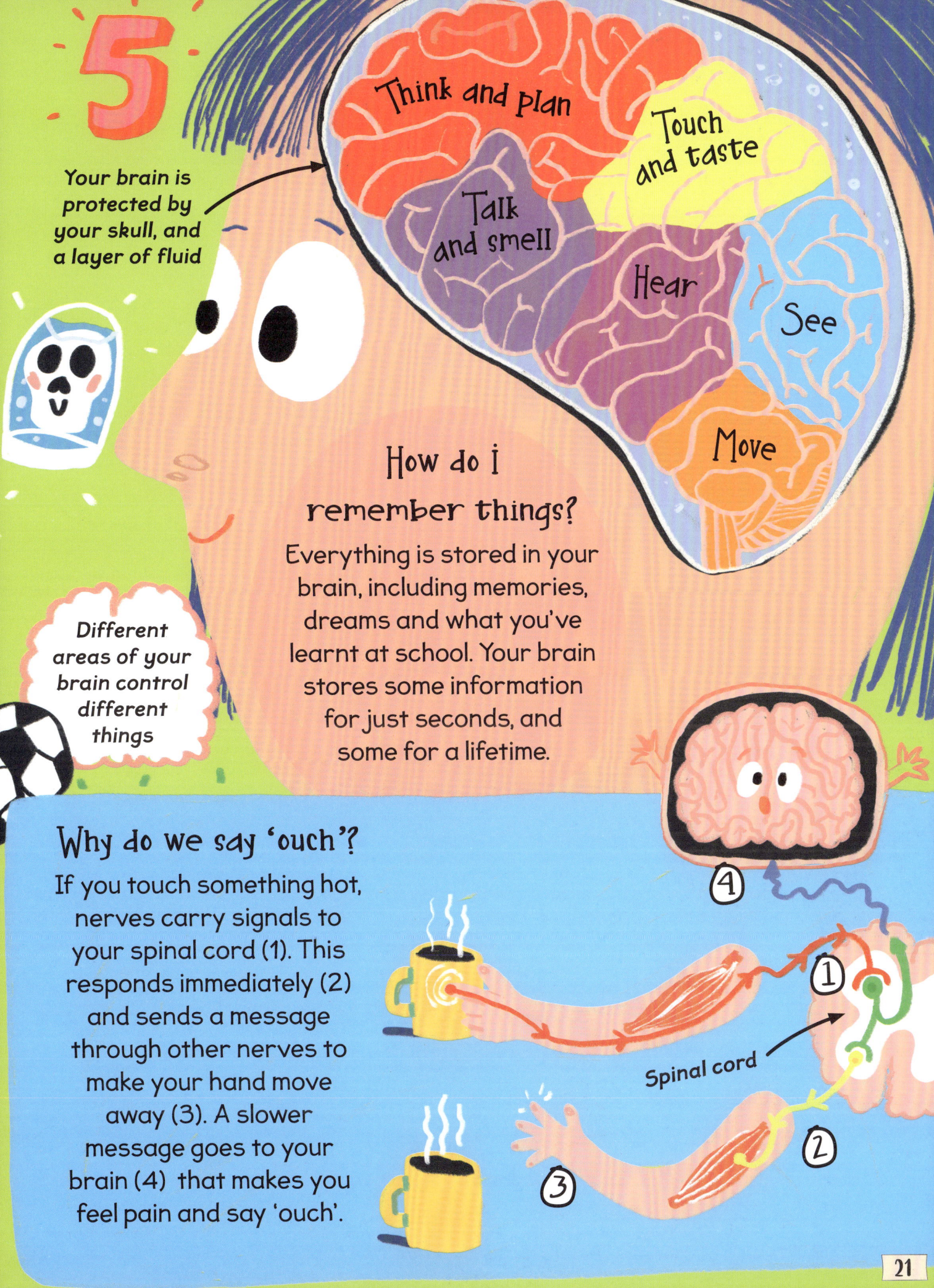

5

Your brain is protected by your skull, and a layer of fluid

Think and plan
Touch and taste
Talk and smell
Hear
See
Move

How do I remember things?

Everything is stored in your brain, including memories, dreams and what you've learnt at school. Your brain stores some information for just seconds, and some for a lifetime.

Different areas of your brain control different things

Why do we say 'ouch'?

If you touch something hot, nerves carry signals to your spinal cord (1). This responds immediately (2) and sends a message through other nerves to make your hand move away (3). A slower message goes to your brain (4) that makes you feel pain and say 'ouch'.

Spinal cord

21

Why do I sleep?

Your body uses the time you're asleep to repair any injuries, grow, rest and sort out what you've experienced and learnt during the day. No one knows exactly how sleep works, but we do know that we can't live without it.

Does everyone dream?

Yes, but not everyone remembers their dreams. Most people have 3-5 dreams each night. Even cats and dogs have dreams!

No one knows what animals dream about!

Would you rather?

Be able to breathe underwater or be **light** enough to walk on top of the water?

Have a really long **tongue** or really long **fingers**?

Have **super-keen sight** or be able to hear very **quiet sounds** like ants munching their food?

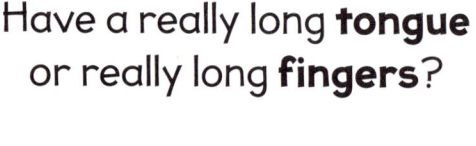

Grow really long **fingernails** or really **long hair**?

Have **unbreakable** bones or **uncuttable** skin?

Have **wings** or a **tail**?

Be **wobbly** like a jellyfish with no bones, or have a **hard** outer shell like a tortoise?

Be entirely **furry** or entirely **bald**?

Have eyes in the back of your **head** or in the tips of your **fingers**?

Be able to run really **fast** or for a really **long** time?

Where do babies come from?

Babies come from inside their mum's body. A baby grows in the mum's uterus, where it gets everything it needs until it's ready to be born.

Cord

Uterus

I can feel the baby kicking!

Goodness from the mother's food is carried along the cord to the baby

Egg cell divides again and again

Day 1

Day 2

Days 3–4

How fast does a baby grow?

Inside its mum, a baby grows really fast. It starts off as a tiny egg, which divides to make the billions of cells that make up the whole baby. After nine months, the baby is big enough to be born.

12 weeks
5 centimetres

20 weeks
16 centimetres

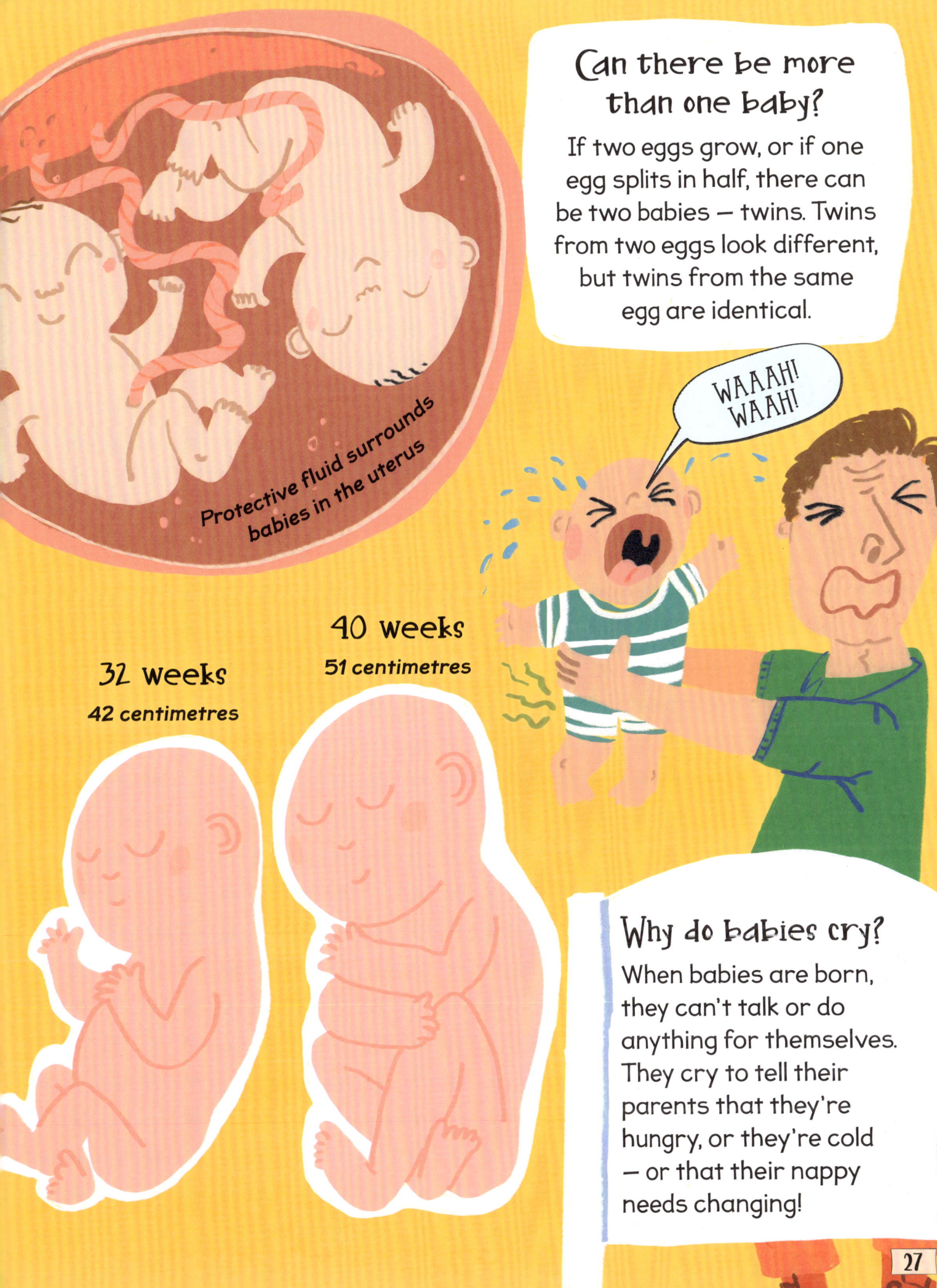

Can there be more than one baby?

If two eggs grow, or if one egg splits in half, there can be two babies — twins. Twins from two eggs look different, but twins from the same egg are identical.

Protective fluid surrounds babies in the uterus

32 weeks
42 centimetres

40 weeks
51 centimetres

WAAAH! WAAH!

Why do babies cry?

When babies are born, they can't talk or do anything for themselves. They cry to tell their parents that they're hungry, or they're cold — or that their nappy needs changing!

Am I always growing?

You keep growing from when you are born until your late teens or early twenties. But the speed you grow at slows down. A baby triples its weight in a year.

Do you know how tall you are?

Babies double their weight in five months. If you kept doing that you'd be huge!

5 years

6 months

Newborn

10 years

How do I get taller?

A soft, flexible substance called cartilage grows inside your bones, making them longer. The cartilage slowly hardens into bone.

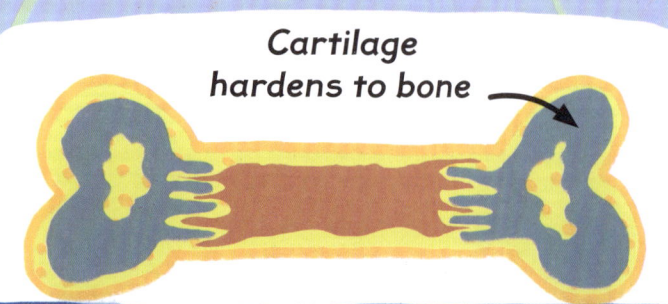

Cartilage hardens to bone

Why does my hair need cutting?

Your hair grows throughout your life, so you have to keep cutting it. Hair grows from a little pit on your scalp called a hair follicle, but the hair you can see is actually dead. That's why it doesn't hurt to have a haircut.

Hair follicle

15 years

20 years

70 years

Your ears keep getting bigger too, but very slowly.

Grandma? Grandpa?

Do we shrink as we get older?

Yes! The bones of the spine get squashed closer together over the years. Some older people also get a curved spine and stoop, and that makes them look even shorter.

A compendium of questions

Why do my first teeth fall out?

Your first teeth are temporary — you have them until your mouth grows large enough for your permanent teeth. You have 20 first teeth, and they are replaced by larger, stronger, teeth.

What are hiccups?

If the muscle across your chest suddenly squeezes, it can snap shut the opening to your vocal flaps, making the 'hic' sound.

Why do we like sugar if it's bad for us?

Millions of years ago, our ancestors ate a sugar-rich fruit diet. So gradually people grew to like sweet things.

Why do I yawn?

No one's quite sure, but possibly as a way of getting more oxygen into your body quickly.

What are goosebumps?

They are bumps on your skin where tiny muscles make your hairs stand up if you are cold or scared.

Why do we get wrinkles?

As skin ages, it loses its elasticity, so it can't spring back into shape after stretching (such as when you smile).

Why don't I have to remember to breathe?

Your brain deals with all kinds of automatic activities without you having to think about them, including breathing, and digesting food.

What is my tummy button for?

When you were inside your mother, you got nutrients and oxygen through the umbilical cord that connected you to her body. The tummy button is what's left after the cord is cut.

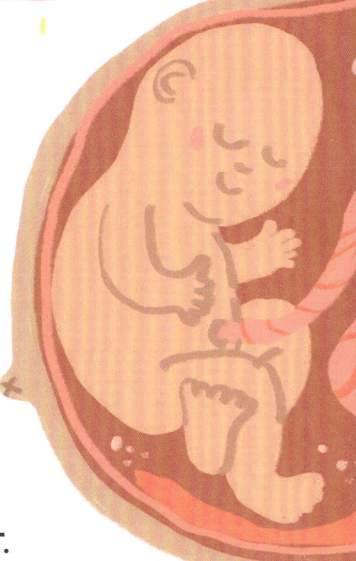

Why is blood red?

Blood contains a chemical for carrying oxygen that contains iron. When this chemical picks up oxygen, it turns redder.

What makes a scab?

When your blood meets the air, special cells called platelets break up and mix with a protein in blood to make tangly fibres, forming a scab.

Why do I sleep more when I'm ill?

Your body needs energy to fight the illness, so to save energy it makes you sleep.